101 F
ABOUT BILLIE
EILISH

The Unofficial Kid and Teen Quiz & Trivia Guide to the Amazing Popstar

Tessa Temecula

1: Billie Was Born Into a Family of Musicians

Billie Eilish was born in Los Angeles on December 18, 2001, into a family passionate about the arts. Both of her parents, Maggie Baird and Patrick O'Connell, are musicians and actors. They encouraged Billie and her brother Finneas to express themselves through creativity from a very young age. Their home was filled with music, and it's no surprise that both siblings pursued successful careers in the music industry.

2: Billie's Full Name Has a Unique Story Behind It

Billie Eilish's full name is Billie Eilish Pirate Baird O'Connell, and each part of her name carries a special meaning. She was named after her maternal grandfather, Bill Baird, who passed away before she was born. "Eilish" is the Irish version of Elizabeth, and "Pirate" was suggested by her older brother Finneas when he was just a little boy, and it stuck! Her last name, O'Connell, comes from her father's side of the family.

3: She Started Writing Songs at Age 11

Billie Eilish began writing music when she was just 11 years old. Her very first song was inspired by The Walking Dead, a show she was obsessed with at the time. The song was about a zombie apocalypse, and her love of storytelling in songwriting was born. With help from her brother Finneas, Billie's songwriting skills developed quickly, leading to the creation of some of her biggest hits just a few years later.

4: Billie's Brother Finneas Is Her Main Collaborator

Billie's older brother, Finneas O'Connell, is not just her sibling but also her creative partner. The two have worked together on nearly every song she has released, with Finneas writing, producing, and playing instruments on her tracks. Their strong bond allows them to make music that feels personal and authentic, which has helped Billie stand out in the music world.

5: She Was Homeschooled

Billie didn't attend traditional school like most kids. Instead, she was homeschooled by her mother, Maggie Baird, along with her brother Finneas. This allowed Billie to have a more flexible schedule and focus on her passions for music, dance, and art. The homeschooling environment gave her the freedom to dive into her creative interests, which played a huge role in shaping her career.

6: "Ocean Eyes" Was Her Breakout Hit

In 2015, Billie and Finneas uploaded her song "Ocean Eyes" to SoundCloud, expecting it to be just another small project. But the song went viral almost immediately, with listeners falling in love with Billie's haunting vocals and emotional lyrics. The track was originally written by Finneas for his band, but once Billie recorded it, they knew it was something special. "Ocean Eyes" launched Billie's career and marked the beginning of her rise to fame.

7: Billie's Signature Style Is All About Comfort

Billie Eilish is known for her oversized, baggy clothing, which has become her signature look. While her unique style has been praised for breaking the mold of typical pop star fashion, Billie has shared that her choice of clothing is all about comfort and wanting to control how she is perceived. She's spoken openly about how her fashion allows her to feel more confident and free from judgment about her body.

8: Billie Became the Youngest Artist to Win the Big Four Grammys

In 2020, Billie Eilish made history at the Grammy Awards by becoming the youngest artist ever to win the four major categories in the same year: Album of the Year, Record of the Year, Song of the Year, and Best New Artist. At 18 years old, she won these prestigious awards for her debut album When We All Fall Asleep, Where Do We Go? and its hit single "Bad Guy." This cemented her status as a major force in the music industry.

Did you know?

9: She Has a Love for Spooky and Dark Imagery

Billie Eilish is known for incorporating eerie and dark themes into her music and visuals. She has always been fascinated by horror movies, dreams, and the idea of facing fears. Her album When We All Fall Asleep, Where Do We Go? is filled with dreamlike, sometimes creepy imagery, and her music videos often play with haunting visuals. Billie's unique style has made her one of the most distinctive voices in pop music today.

10: Billie Is Vegan and Passionate About Animal Rights

Billie Eilish has been a committed vegan since she was 12 years old, and her choice stems from a deep love and concern for animals. Over the years, she has used her immense platform to raise awareness about animal cruelty, often speaking out on the importance of ethical treatment of animals. Through social media posts, interviews, and collaborations with organizations, Billie encourages her fans to consider adopting plant-based diets, highlighting the positive impact it can have on both animals and the environment.

11: Billie Directed Her Own Music Video for "Xanny"

In 2019, Billie made her directorial debut with the music video for her song "Xanny" from her album When We All Fall Asleep, Where Do We Go?. The video features minimalistic visuals, with Billie sitting on a bench while multiple hands extinguish cigarettes on her face. The eerie, slow-paced video perfectly complements the song's theme, and Billie took control of every aspect. She's expressed how important it is for her to be involved in the creative direction of her work, and this marked a major step in her career as a visual artist.

12: Billie Has Tourette Syndrome

Billie Eilish has openly shared that she has Tourette syndrome, a neurological disorder that causes involuntary movements and sounds called tics. She was diagnosed with Tourette syndrome when she was 11 years old, and she's been candid about her experiences with the condition. While it doesn't affect her singing or performances, Billie has said that she experiences tics daily. By speaking out, she hopes to raise awareness and encourage others to embrace their differences.

Show Off Your Billie Smarts!

1. What was Billie Eilish's debut single that went viral on SoundCloud?

A) Ocean Eyes
B) Bad Guy
C) Bellyache
D) Lovely

2. Which family member does Billie collaborate with on her music?
A) Her sister
B) Her mother
C) Her cousin
D) Her brother Finneas

3. In which year did Billie Eilish release her debut album When We All Fall Asleep, Where Do We Go??

A) 2017
B) 2018
C) 2019
D) 2020

13: Billie also has Has Synesthesia

Alongside Tourette syndrome, Billie has also revealed that she has synesthesia, a condition where senses are crossed in unusual ways. For Billie, this means she can "see" music as colors and shapes. This unique way of experiencing the world has influenced her creative process, and she often associates specific colors with certain songs or emotions. It's one of the reasons her music and visuals feel so distinct and immersive.

14: Her Brother Finneas Is Also a Successful Solo Artist

While Billie is best known for her collaborations with her brother Finneas, who produces much of her music, Finneas has also built an impressive solo career. He's released several singles and an album, Blood Harmony, that highlight his singer-songwriter abilities. Though he's earned multiple awards for his work with Billie, Finneas has carved out his own path as a solo artist, proving that talent runs deep in the O'Connell family. His work continues to gain recognition, both with Billie and on his own.

15: Billie Released a Book of Personal Photographs

In 2021, Billie published a book titled Billie Eilish, packed with never-before-seen photographs from her life. The book gives fans an intimate look into her world, covering everything from childhood memories to behind-the-scenes moments in her career. Billie was personally involved in the project, carefully selecting the photos and sharing insights into her journey from a young girl in Los Angeles to a global superstar. With her growing list of accomplishments, we have to wonder—could her next book be an autobiography?

16: Billie Is a Huge Justin Bieber Fan

Growing up, Billie Eilish was a massive fan of Justin Bieber. She's mentioned in interviews how much she loved his music, even covering her walls with posters of him. When her own career skyrocketed, Billie finally got to meet Justin at Coachella in 2019—a dream come true. The two hit it off and later collaborated on a remix of her hit song "Bad Guy." Billie has called the experience of working with her childhood idol both surreal and incredibly exciting, a full-circle moment she never could have imagined when she was just a kid with posters on her wall.

17: She Wrote "Everything I Wanted" About Her Struggles with Fame

Billie's song "Everything I Wanted" was written with her brother Finneas and dives deep into the pressures and challenges that come with fame. In the lyrics, Billie reflects on how overwhelming her rise to stardom has been, sharing the feeling of being disconnected from the life she knew before fame took over. The song became a huge hit, connecting with fans who appreciate its raw honesty and vulnerability. It's a powerful reminder that even in the spotlight, the weight of fame can be heavy, but Billie's openness has always resonated with her listeners.

18: Billie Became a Global Sensation Before Ever Releasing an Album

Before her debut album, When We All Fall Asleep, Where Do We Go? was released, Billie Eilish had already gained millions of fans worldwide through her singles and E.P. Don't Smile at Me. Songs like "Ocean Eyes" and "Bellyache" helped her build a strong following, and by the time her album dropped, Billie was already a global sensation. Her ability to connect with fans before even releasing a full album was a testament to her unique sound and personality.

19: Billie Has a Love for Horror Movies

Billie Eilish has always been a big fan of horror films, and if you've seen her music videos, it totally shows! She loves that thrilling, heart-racing feeling that comes from being scared, and it plays a huge part in her creative process. Whether it's the eerie visuals in her "Bury a Friend" video or the haunting themes in her album When We All Fall Asleep, Where Do We Go?, her love for all things spooky shines through. It's almost like Billie turns her fascination with fear into art, making her music and visuals feel both thrilling and a little chilling.

20: Billie Voiced a Character on "The Simpsons"

In 2022, Billie Eilish made a fun guest appearance on The Simpsons, voicing herself in a special episode called "When Billie Met Lisa." In the episode, Billie finds out that Lisa Simpson is an amazing saxophone player, and the two team up for a jam session. It was an exciting collaboration for Billie, especially since she's been a huge fan of the iconic show for years. This crossover not only gave fans a fun moment but also showed how Billie's influence reaches way beyond the music scene and into pop culture.

Did you know?

21: Billie Has a Pet Dog Named Shark

Billie Eilish is a huge animal lover. In 2020, she adopted a gray pit bull rescue dog named Shark. Shark often appears on Billie's social media and is known for his sweet and calm demeanor. Billie has spoken about how important Shark is to her, helping her feel grounded amidst the chaos of her busy career. Shark is often by Billie's side during her downtime, offering a much-needed sense of comfort and companionship.

22: She Was the Youngest Female to Headline Coachella

In 2022, Billie Eilish made history as the youngest female artist to ever headline Coachella at just 20 years old. Her performance was packed with energy, creativity, and an undeniable connection with the audience, leaving fans in awe. Being at the center of such an iconic festival was a huge milestone for Billie, marking her as not just a pop sensation but a powerhouse performer. Her Coachella set further solidified her place as one of the biggest stars in the music world, showing everyone that she's just getting started.

23: Billie Released Her First Song at Age 14

Billie Eilish was only 14 when she dropped her debut single, "Ocean Eyes," on SoundCloud. Her brother, Finneas, wrote and produced the track, originally intended for a dance class, but it quickly became something much bigger. The song went viral almost overnight, racking up millions of streams and putting Billie on the radar of major record labels. That early success was the spark that launched her remarkable journey in the music industry, setting the stage for her rise to global stardom. Pretty wild for a song meant for a dance routine, right?

24: Billie Is Known for Her Baggy, Oversized Fashion

Billie Eilish has made a name for herself as a fashion icon with her signature oversized, baggy clothing style. She's explained that dressing this way makes her feel more comfortable and lets her express herself without being judged based on her body. By rocking her own look, Billie has inspired countless fans to embrace their individuality and push back against traditional beauty standards. Her style isn't just about clothes—it's about self-confidence and freedom to be yourself, no matter what anyone else thinks.

Show Off Your Billie Smarts!

4. What is the name of the James Bond theme song Billie Eilish wrote and performed?

A) GoldenEye
B) No Time to Die
C) Skyfall
D) Writing on the Wall

5. Which award did Billie Eilish win for the song No Time to Die?

A) Golden Globe
B) Academy Award
C) Emmy Award
D) Tony Award

6. What is Billie Eilish's middle name?

A) Pirate
B) Pearl
C) Violet
D) Rose

25: She Won an Oscar for the James Bond Song "No Time to Die"

In 2022, Billie Eilish took home the Academy Award for Best Original Song for "No Time to Die," the James Bond theme she wrote and performed. This win made her the youngest artist ever to receive an Oscar for a Bond theme, adding yet another major accolade to her growing list of achievements. It was a huge moment for Billie, who continues to break records and prove that her talent knows no limits, whether it's in the studio or on one of Hollywood's biggest stages.

26: Billie Collaborated with Rosalia for "Lo Vas A Olvidar"

In 2021, Billie Eilish teamed up with Spanish singer Rosalía for the haunting track "Lo Vas A Olvidar," featured on the soundtrack for HBO's hit show Euphoria. The song, performed mostly in Spanish, highlighted Billie's versatility, allowing her to effortlessly explore different genres and languages. This collaboration was a massive success, bringing Billie's music to new audiences worldwide and further proving her ability to adapt and innovate across the global music scene.

27: Billie Eilish Had a Swimsuit Controversy in 2020

In 2020, Billie made headlines when she shared a rare photo of herself in a swimsuit during a vacation. Known for her typically baggy and oversized clothing, the image sparked an intense reaction from fans and the media. Billie later addressed the situation, expressing frustration over how much focus is placed on women's bodies and how she chooses to dress. This moment became significant in the conversation about body positivity and self-acceptance.

28: Billie Is the Youngest Person to Win All Four Major Grammy Categories in the Same Year

At the 2020 Grammy Awards, Billie Eilish made history by becoming the youngest artist to win all four major categories: Best New Artist, Record of the Year, Song of the Year, and Album of the Year. She was just 18 years old at the time. Billie's sweeping victory that night cemented her place in music history and marked her as one of the most influential artists of her generation.

29: Billie Has a Love for Skateboarding

In addition to her passion for music, Billie Eilish has a long-standing love for skateboarding. Growing up in Los Angeles, she often spent time at skate parks honing her skills, and this hobby became a creative outlet outside of her musical career. Billie has mentioned how skateboarding helps her clear her mind and de-stress, offering a fun break from her busy schedule. While she may not hit the skate park as often due to her packed career, her love for the sport remains a key part of her personality

30: Billie Was Homeschooled by Her Parents

Billie Eilish and her brother Finneas were homeschooled by their parents, allowing them to explore their creative interests at an early age. Billie has said that homeschooling gave her the freedom to focus on her passions, like singing and songwriting, without the constraints of a traditional school schedule. This unconventional education played a huge role in shaping Billie's unique approach to her music and creativity.

Did you know?

31: Billie Eilish Started Her Own Perfume Line

In 2021, Billie Eilish ventured into the fragrance industry with the release of her debut perfume, simply titled "Eilish." The scent, which is vegan and cruelty-free, was a personal project for Billie, as she has a deep connection to different smells and believes that fragrance is a powerful part of self-expression. Her perfume quickly became a bestseller, and fans loved the warm, vanilla-based scent that Billie herself said reflected her identity.

32: Billie Eilish Directed Her Own Music Video at 17

At just 17 years old, Billie Eilish made her directorial debut with the music video for her song "Xanny." Taking full creative control, Billie directed and starred in the video, shaping every aspect of its creation. The minimalist yet striking visuals feature Billie sitting still while cigarette burns appear on her skin, symbolizing the damaging effects of smoking and addiction. The haunting imagery aligned with the song's message, making it a powerful statement. This project marked the start of Billie taking an even bigger role in her creative direction, giving fans a glimpse of her artistic vision beyond just the music.

33: She Often Struggled with Body Image Issues

Billie Eilish has been open about her struggles with body image, particularly during her teenage years. In interviews, she shared that the pressure of being in the public eye often made her uncomfortable with how people focused on her appearance rather than her music. Billie's decision to wear oversized clothing stemmed from a desire to control how much of her body the world would see, giving her a sense of empowerment in an industry that often judges women for their looks.

34: Billie Was Featured on the Soundtrack for Pixar's Turning Red

In 2022, Billie Eilish and her brother Finneas collaborated on the soundtrack for Pixar's animated film Turning Red. They wrote and produced several songs for the fictional boy band 4*Town, including the catchy hits "Nobody Like U" and "1 True Love." The movie's nostalgic early-2000s vibe paired perfectly with Billie and Finneas's songwriting style, and their involvement helped make the soundtrack a fan favorite.

Did you know?

35: She Had a Cameo in Donald Glover's Swarm Series

In 2023, Billie Eilish made her acting debut with a cameo in Donald Glover's Amazon Prime series Swarm. She took on the role of Eva, a manipulative cult leader, in a performance that earned her praise from critics. Billie's portrayal of the eerie, unsettling character was a standout, showcasing her range and proving that her talents go far beyond music. Fans were impressed by how naturally she stepped into the world of acting, making many wonder if this could be the start of more on-screen roles in her future.

36: Billie's First Album Was Inspired by Nightmares

Billie Eilish's debut album When We All Fall Asleep, Where Do We Go? was deeply influenced by her fascination with dreams and nightmares. Songs like the haunting "Bury a Friend" capture the dark, eerie themes that run throughout the album. Billie has shared that the title was inspired by her own experiences with sleep paralysis and vivid nightmares, which have long fueled her creativity. This blend of personal fears and surreal imagery shaped the album's unique atmosphere, making it one of the most memorable debuts in recent music history.

Show Off Your Billie Smarts!

7. Which iconic pop artist inspired Billie to pursue music?

A) Madonna
B) Britney Spears
C) Justin Bieber
D) Taylor Swift

8. Billie Eilish became the youngest artist to headline which major music festival?

A) Lollapalooza
B) Glastonbury
C) Coachella
D) Bonnaroo

9. What was the title of Billie's second studio album?

A) Don't Smile at Me
B) Happier Than Ever
C) Ocean Eyes
D) Bellyache

Did you know?

37: She Was Heavily Influenced by Hip-Hop and R&B

Though Billie Eilish's music is often categorized as pop, she has always cited hip-hop and R&B as some of her biggest influences. Artists like Tyler, the Creator, and Childish Gambino have shaped Billie's approach to songwriting and production, and her music often incorporates elements of these genres. Billie's ability to blend pop with hip-hop beats and R&B rhythms gives her music a unique, genre-defying sound.

38: Billie Loves Writing Music While Traveling

Billie Eilish has shared that she often finds her best song ideas while traveling. Whether she's on a plane, in a car, or moving from one city to another, the constant change of scenery sparks her creativity in ways a stationary environment can't. Many of her biggest hits were written while on tour or visiting new places, as the energy and atmosphere of different locations provide fresh inspiration. For Billie, the movement itself seems to unlock a flow of ideas, turning everyday travel into a powerful creative process.

39: Billie Collaborated with Takashi Murakami for Fashion

In 2019, Billie Eilish partnered with renowned Japanese artist Takashi Murakami for a unique clothing collection that blended her signature oversized streetwear style with Murakami's bold and playful artwork. The limited-edition pieces, featuring eye-catching designs and vibrant colors, were an instant hit and sold out quickly. This collaboration not only showcased Billie's influence in the fashion world but also highlighted her ability to merge art and style in a way that resonates with fans. It was yet another milestone in her journey to becoming a global fashion icon.

40: Billie Eilish Has a Collection of Unique Jewelry Pieces

Billie Eilish has an eye for bold, unique jewelry, and she's often seen wearing chunky rings, layered necklaces, and statement pieces that complement her edgy style. One of her favorite accessories is a custom-made ring that spells out her name, a piece she's often spotted with at events. Billie has said that jewelry allows her to express herself in a personal way, and it's become a significant part of her overall aesthetic. Her collection is a reflection of her individualism and her desire to stand out, both in fashion and in music.

41: Billie Eilish Won a Guinness World Record for Her James Bond Theme Song

In 2020, Billie Eilish made history when her song "No Time to Die" for the James Bond film of the same name became the first Bond theme to top the U.K. charts. This achievement earned Billie a Guinness World Record, making her the youngest artist to write and perform a James Bond theme song. The haunting ballad went on to win both a Grammy and an Academy Award, further establishing Billie as one of the most successful young artists in the music industry.

42: Billie Eilish Designed a Signature Ukulele

In 2020, Billie Eilish collaborated with Fender to release a custom-designed ukulele. The instrument was a special nod to her early years of playing music, as Billie began learning the ukulele at just six years old. The design of the ukulele features her signature "blohsh" symbol and comes in a sleek black finish, reflecting her personal style. Billie has shared that the ukulele is one of her favorite instruments, and she hopes her signature model will inspire more young people to pick up the instrument and start making music.

43: Billie Eilish Wrote a Song for Pixar's Turning Red

In 2022, Billie and her brother Finneas got the chance to dive into the nostalgic world of early 2000s pop music when they contributed three original songs to Pixar's animated movie Turning Red. The songs were performed by the fictional boy band 4*Town and totally nailed that fun, boy band sound from back in the day. Billie has said she had a blast working on the project, as it brought back memories of the music she loved growing up. It's like she got to relive her childhood playlist—but this time, as the songwriter behind it!

44: Billie's First Tour Was with Florence and the Machine

Before headlining her own world tours, Billie Eilish opened for Florence and the Machine on their High as Hope tour in 2018. This experience was crucial for Billie's growth as a live performer, and she credits Florence Welch as a major influence on her stage presence and musical style. Touring with such a legendary band gave Billie early exposure to massive audiences. It helped her gain confidence as a rising star.

Did you know?

45: Billie Has a Deep Fear of Needles

Despite her edgy persona, Billie Eilish has admitted to being terrified of needles. She has spoken candidly about her fear of getting blood tests and vaccines, which is something she has struggled with since childhood. Despite this fear, Billie has publicly supported vaccination efforts, especially during the COVID-19 pandemic, encouraging her fans to get vaccinated while acknowledging that it can be tough for those who share her phobia.

46: Billie Eilish Once Broke an Apple Music Record for Pre-Adds

In 2021, Billie Eilish made history by breaking an Apple Music record with her album Happier Than Ever. The album set the record for the most pre-adds ever on the platform, with over 1 million people adding the album to their libraries before its official release. This showed the massive anticipation for her sophomore album and how deeply her fanbase connects with her music. The excitement surrounding the release cemented her as one of the most influential artists of her generation.

47: Billie Eilish Once Recorded a Song in Her Childhood Bedroom

A fun fact about Billie Eilish is that she recorded some of her biggest early songs, including Ocean Eyes, in her childhood bedroom. Alongside her brother Finneas, they used a basic setup to create what would become viral hits. This humble, DIY approach to music production is a testament to their creativity and bond as siblings. Even after achieving fame, Billie has mentioned how those early home recording sessions remain a cherished part of her musical journey.

48: She Was Heavily Inspired by Lana Del Rey

Billie Eilish has openly credited Lana Del Rey as one of her biggest musical influences. Billie has admired Lana's melancholic, cinematic sound and her ability to convey deep emotions through her music. This influence can be seen in Billie's own music, which often features moody, introspective lyrics and dreamy, atmospheric production. The two artists share a similar ability to create vivid emotional landscapes in their songs.

Show Off Your Billie Smarts!

10. In which city did Billie Eilish grow up?

A) New York
B) Chicago
C) San Francisco
D) Los Angeles

11. Billie Eilish has spoken publicly about her diagnosis. Which condition has she been diagnosed with?

A) ADHD
B) Tourette syndrome
C) OCD
D) Anxiety disorder

12. Billie's brother Finneas is a successful musician in his own right. What is his stage name?

A) Fin
B) Finneas
C) O'Connell
D) Phoenix

49: Billie Once Performed with Her Childhood Idol, Justin Bieber

Billie Eilish was a huge fan of Justin Bieber growing up, and one of her dreams came true when she collaborated with him on a remix of her hit song "Bad Guy." The collaboration was a full-circle moment for Billie, who had idolized Bieber since she was a child. She later performed with him at Coachella, marking a special milestone in her career and fulfilling a long-held dream of working with her musical hero.

50: Billie Eilish Struggled with Depression as a Teenager

Billie Eilish has been open about her struggles with mental health, including depression and anxiety, particularly during her teenage years. At the height of her early fame, Billie experienced intense pressure and feelings of isolation, which led to bouts of depression. She has used her platform to talk about the importance of mental health awareness, and many of her songs, such as "Everything I Wanted," reflect her personal experiences with these challenges.

Did you know?

51: She's a Guinness World Record Holder for the Youngest Artist with Multiple Grammy Wins

At the 2020 Grammy Awards, Billie Eilish became the youngest artist in history to win not just one but four of the most prestigious categories: Album of the Year, Record of the Year, Song of the Year, and Best New Artist. This historic achievement made her a Guinness World Record holder, cementing her place in music history by the time she was just 18 years old.

52: Billie Loves Vintage Fashion and High-End Streetwear

Though she's known for her signature oversized clothing, Billie Eilish deeply loves fashion and often mixes high-end streetwear with vintage styles. She's been seen wearing brands like Gucci, Burberry, and Louis Vuitton while frequently shopping at thrift stores for unique pieces. Billie's eclectic style has made her a fashion icon for the younger generation, embracing individuality and comfort in what she wears.

53: Billie Eilish Is a Huge Fan of The Office

Billie has mentioned on several occasions that The Office is one of her all-time favorite T.V. shows. In fact, her song "My Strange Addiction" features audio clips from the show. She once even had a special moment where she got to meet Rainn Wilson, who plays Dwight Schrute, and he quizzed her on trivia from the series. Billie's love for The Office shows just how relatable she is to her fans, who also enjoy binge-watching iconic shows.

54: She Wrote a Song at Just 11 Years Old Inspired by The Walking Dead

One of Billie's earliest songwriting efforts was inspired by the popular T.V. series The Walking Dead. At just 11 years old, Billie wrote a song about the zombie apocalypse, reflecting her creative mind from a young age. She mentioned that the song took lines from the show and captured the dark and eerie tone that fans of her music have come to love.

Did you know?

55: Billie's Love for Horror Influences Her Music Videos

Billie Eilish has a deep love for horror, and this influence is clear in many of her music videos. The eerie visuals in videos like "Bury a Friend" and "All the Good Girls Go to Hell" feature elements inspired by classic horror movies and dark themes. Billie has said that the unsettling atmosphere in these videos is meant to reflect the deeper emotional struggles that her music often addresses.

56: Billie Eilish Loves to Collect Strange Souvenirs

Billie Eilish has a quirky habit of collecting unique and unusual souvenirs during her travels. Instead of typical tourist trinkets, she gravitates toward odd or unconventional items. Whether it's something vintage, peculiar, or slightly eerie, Billie enjoys finding treasures that match her unique sense of style and interests. This fun hobby gives fans another peek into her eclectic personality and love for the unconventional.

57: Billie's Middle Name "Pirate" Was Her Brother's Idea

Billie's full name is Billie Eilish Pirate Baird O'Connell, and the unique middle name "Pirate" was actually suggested by her brother, Finneas, when he was young. Originally, her parents planned to name her "Eilish Pirate O'Connell." Still, after her grandfather passed away before she was born, they honored him by naming her Billie after him while keeping "Pirate" as her middle name.

58: Billie's Synesthesia Helps Shape Her Music

Billie Eilish has synesthesia, which means her senses mix in a way that lets her "see" sounds as colors. So, when she's making music, she's not just hearing it—she's visualizing it too! Imagine listening to a song and seeing a wave of colors wash over you—that's what Billie experiences. This unique ability plays a big role in how she writes and produces her tracks, often connecting certain emotions with specific colors. It's one of the reasons her music feels so vivid and her visuals are so striking. Pretty cool to think that her songs are like a painting she's creating with sound!

59: Billie Eilish Has a Love for Video Games

Billie Eilish is a huge fan of video games and often talks about her love for gaming in interviews. She has mentioned that video games were a big part of her childhood, and she still enjoys playing in her free time. Some of her favorites include classics like The Legend of Zelda: Breath of the Wild and Animal Crossing. Billie has even credited gaming with helping her relax and decompress after long tours or recording sessions. It's a hobby that many of her fans share, making her even more relatable.

60: Billie Eilish Has a Love for Cars, Especially Vintage Ones

While many fans know Billie for her music and unique style, few might be aware of her passion for cars, especially vintage ones. Billie has expressed her fascination with classic vehicles, often admiring their design and aesthetics. In interviews, she has mentioned that she dreams of owning a collection of vintage cars someday. This interest adds another layer to her personality, showing that her love for creativity extends beyond just music and fashion—it reaches into the world of automotive beauty too!

13. Which song became a viral dance trend on TikTok?

A) Bad Guy
B) Therefore, I Am
C) Bury a Friend
D) You Should See Me in a Crown

14. What is the title of Billie Eilish's book, which features a collection of personal photos and stories?

A) My Life in Photos
B) By - Billie Eilish
C) Billie: The Story
D) Through My Eyes

15. How old was Billie released her first single, Ocean Eyes?

A) 14
B) 15
C) 16
D) 17

Did you know?

61: Billie Eilish Collects Unusual Items

Did you know that Billie Eilish has a quirky passion for collecting vintage toys and odd trinkets? Her collection includes everything from old dolls to funky, one-of-a-kind items that catch her eye. It's a fun hobby that really shows off her creative and playful side. Imagine what kind of cool, unusual things you might find in her collection! What would you add to your own collection if you had the chance? Maybe something that reminds you of your childhood or something totally unique, just like Billie!

62: She Once Performed at the Democratic National Convention

Billie Eilish used her platform to encourage young fans to vote in the 2020 U.S. Presidential Election. She performed her song "My Future" at the Democratic National Convention, showcasing her music and delivering a powerful message urging viewers to get involved in the political process. Billie's active role in political conversations demonstrates her commitment to using her voice for more than just music.

63: Billie Eilish Writes from the Heart

Billie Eilish is all about keeping it real in her music. Many of her songs, like "Everything I Wanted," dive into personal experiences—her struggles with self-doubt and the pressures of fame. But that's not all! She often tackles topics like mental health, relationships, and personal growth, which is why her lyrics feel so relatable to so many people. Her music connects with fans on a deep level. Can you think of a song that speaks to your own feelings or experiences? Maybe it's one of Billie's tracks or another artist who hits you right in the heart.

64: Billie Eilish Has a Spider Collection

Did you know Billie Eilish isn't just into music and fashion—she also has a love for spiders? Billie has shared that she finds spiders fascinating and even had a tarantula crawl on her face in the music video for "You Should See Me in a Crown." While some people might be creeped out, Billie embraces her interest in these eight-legged creatures. Would you ever be brave enough to hold a spider like Billie?

65: Billie's Voice Was Featured in Diary of a Wimpy Kid

Before Billie Eilish became the pop sensation we know today, she had a surprising early gig in the world of movies! Billie provided ADR (additional dialogue recording) for the movie Diary of a Wimpy Kid: Rodrick Rules. While her voice acting career didn't take off like her music did, it's still a fun little-known fact about her early days in the entertainment industry. It just goes to show how multi-talented Billie is, even from a young age. Imagine—if music hadn't worked out, maybe we'd be seeing her in more films! Can you picture Billie voicing more characters in movies?

66: Billie Eilish Used to Be a Competitive Dancer

Before Billie Eilish became a global music sensation, she was actually a competitive dancer! She took dance classes for many years and performed in a variety of styles, including hip-hop and contemporary. Her dance background has influenced her performances and even inspired some of her songs. In fact, her breakout hit "Ocean Eyes" was originally written for her dance class. Imagine Billie busting out some moves before she took over the music world! Would you like to see her dance in one of her music videos?

67: Billie Eilish Has a Love for Stickers

Believe it or not, Billie Eilish is a big fan of stickers! She loves collecting them and even decorating things like her water bottles, notebooks, and phone case with all kinds of fun and unique designs. Billie has said that stickers make everything more personal and creative. If you had a collection of Billie's favorite stickers, where would you put them? Maybe even start your own sticker collection to make your things as cool as hers!

68: Billie Eilish Loves Pranking Her Fans

Billie Eilish has a great sense of humor and loves to pull pranks on her fans! Once, she disguised herself in a wig and glasses and pretended to be a fan waiting in line to meet... herself! The fans had no idea it was actually Billie, and when she finally revealed her true identity, everyone was shocked and excited. Imagine meeting your favorite artist and realizing you've been talking to them the whole time in disguise! What kind of prank would you pull if you were in Billie's shoes?

69: Billie Eilish Has a Passion for Collecting Sneakers

Billie Eilish is known for her love of sneakers, and she has an impressive collection of unique and rare shoes. She's collaborated with major brands like Nike to create her own sneaker designs, including eco-friendly options! If you could design a sneaker with Billie, what would it look like? Would it be bold, colorful, or maybe something totally out of the box?

70: She Performed for an Audience of Sharks for a Special Concert

In 2021, Billie Eilish performed a special concert underwater in the middle of a shark tank for the documentary series Fin. The performance was part of a global event to raise awareness about ocean conservation and shark population threats. Billie's unique and courageous performance showed her commitment to environmental causes, and the event raised significant attention to the importance of ocean preservation.

71: Billie Had an Aversion to Being Photographed as a Child

As a child, Billie Eilish often hated being in front of the camera. Despite her current career, where she's regularly photographed and filmed, she's shared that being in photos made her uncomfortable when she was younger. Now, Billie has embraced her role in the spotlight but still prefers to maintain control over her image, a major reason why she started directing many of her own music videos.

72: Billie Eilish Is the First Person Born in the 2000s to Have a No. 1 Album in the U.S.

Can you imagine being the first person born in the 2000s to top the charts? Well, Billie Eilish did just that! When her debut album When We All Fall Asleep, Where Do We Go? hit number one on the U.S. Billboard 200, she made history. Think about it—Billie's music marked a new generation of artists rising to fame, and she became a voice for young people everywhere. If you could create an album, what would its vibe be? Maybe dreamy like Billie's, or something totally different?

Show Off Your Billie Smarts!

16. Billie Eilish made history at the Grammy Awards by winning how many of the top four categories in 2020?

A) Two
B) Three
C) Four
D) Five

17. Billie has often spoken about her love for which retro music genre?

A) Jazz
B) Classic Rock
C) Pop-punk
D) 90s Hip-Hop

18. What is the name of Billie Eilish's dog?

A) Shark
B) Buster
C) Max
D) Pepper

73: She Played Ukulele Before Transitioning to Singing

Did you know Billie Eilish's musical journey started with the ukulele? At just six years old, she picked up the small instrument and started making music. Even though she's now known for her powerful vocals, the ukulele holds a special place in her heart. She even teamed up with Fender to design her own line of ukuleles! Can you picture yourself playing one? What would your first song be on Billie's custom ukulele?

74: Billie Has Her Own Line of Clothing with Freak City

Billie Eilish isn't just a music superstar—she's also a fashion icon. In 2019, she partnered with Freak City, a cool L.A. streetwear brand, to design her own clothing line. It's full of the bold, oversized styles she's famous for, inspiring fans to embrace their individuality. Would you rock Billie's streetwear style? Maybe something oversized and bold, or would you add your own twist to her look?

75: She Struggled with Night Terrors and Sleep Paralysis

Billie Eilish has been open about her struggles with night terrors and sleep paralysis, and those experiences had a huge impact on her music. Her debut album When We All Fall Asleep, Where Do We Go? was directly inspired by her dreams—both the creepy and the surreal. The eerie sound of songs like "Bury a Friend" is a reflection of those scary moments. Have you ever had a nightmare so intense it stuck with you? Imagine turning it into a song like Billie did!

76: Billie Was the Youngest Artist to Win All Four Major Grammy Awards in One Night

How does sweeping the Grammy Awards sound? At just 18 years old, Billie Eilish made history as the youngest artist to win the four major Grammy categories—Best New Artist, Album of the Year, Record of the Year, and Song of the Year—all in one night! Her debut album took the world by storm, and she walked away with armfuls of awards. If you could win one Grammy, what would it be for? Singing, songwriting, or maybe even producing like Billie's brother Finneas?

77: Billie Performed in a Virtual Concert at the Height of the Pandemic

During the COVID-19 pandemic, Billie participated in a special virtual concert called Where Do We Go? The Livestream was designed to connect with fans while live music events were postponed. The concert allowed Billie to perform her songs for fans across the globe, proving that even in challenging times, she could find new ways to bring her music to people.

78: She Once Released a Limited-Edition Vinyl That Sold Out Almost Immediately

How fast do you think a Billie Eilish vinyl would sell out? In 2019, Billie released a special live acoustic album through Jack White's Third Man Records, and it sold out almost instantly! This wasn't just any album—it was a limited-edition vinyl that you could only buy at select stores. Fans went crazy for it, proving just how dedicated they are to owning a piece of Billie's music in physical form. If you could own a limited-edition piece of music history, would you go for one of Billie's vinyls? Maybe you'd even frame it!

79: Billie's Single "My Future" Was Written as a Message of Hope

Imagine writing a song that brings hope to millions during uncertain times. That's exactly what Billie did with her 2020 release, "My Future." The world was going through a lot, but Billie's message was all about self-growth and optimism for what's to come. The song became a beacon of positivity for her fans, encouraging everyone to focus on personal development and to believe in a brighter future. Have you ever listened to a song that gave you hope when you needed it the most?

80: She Often Refers to Her Brother Finneas as Her "Best Friend"

What's better than having a best friend? For Billie, it's having her brother Finneas also be her best friend! Their bond is so tight that she often talks about it in interviews. Beyond just collaborating on music, Billie and Finneas are inseparable, and their close relationship is a key ingredient to their success. Finneas isn't just her brother; he's her biggest supporter and creative partner. Do you have someone in your life who feels like both family and your best friend?

81: Billie Eilish Made the Forbes 30 Under 30 List Twice Before She Turned 20

Can you imagine making it onto Forbes' 30 Under 30 list not once, but twice—before you're even 20 years old? That's exactly what Billie did! Her success in music, from viral hits to award-winning albums, has earned her a spot on this prestigious list, which highlights influential young people changing the world. Not only has she achieved massive success in record time, but her ability to turn her passion into a global phenomenon is nothing short of amazing. How would you feel being recognized for your talents at such a young age?

82: Her Song "When the Party's Over" Was Inspired by Minimalism

Sometimes, less is more. That's exactly what Billie had in mind when she and Finneas created "When the Party's Over." The song is hauntingly beautiful, with its stripped-down sound that focuses on just the essentials: her vocals and a few simple instruments. This minimalist approach makes the song feel intimate and raw, as if Billie is singing directly to you. If you listen closely, you can feel the emotions behind every note. Do you prefer songs that are simple and heartfelt, or do you like more complex arrangements?

Did you know?

83: $25 Million from an Apple TV+ Documentary?

Billie Eilish earned a staggering $25 million from her Apple TV+ documentary The World's a Little Blurry? That's right! The film takes fans behind the scenes, offering a raw and intimate look at her journey to stardom, her creative process, and the emotional highs and lows of her personal life. The documentary resonated with millions, making her story relatable and inspiring to people around the world. It's pretty amazing to think that by just being herself, Billie connected with so many people—and turned that connection into massive success! Imagine sharing your life with the world and earning millions from it!

84: Billie's Music Video for "Bad Guy" Hit 1 Billion Views

How incredible is it to have a music video hit over 1 billion views on YouTube? That's exactly what happened with Billie's "Bad Guy"! The video, with its quirky, fun, and colorful visuals, became an instant hit, showing off Billie's unique style and creativity. Not many artists can say they've reached such a huge milestone at such a young age. Can you imagine creating something that over a billion people around the world have watched? It's no wonder Billie's "Bad Guy" became one of the most iconic videos of her generation!

Show Off Your Billie Smarts!

19. Which Netflix documentary follows Billie's life and career?

A) Billie Eilish: The Journey
B) Happier Than Ever: A Love Story
C) Billie Eilish: The World's a Little Blurry
D) Billie Eilish: Inside Out

20. In which year did Billie Eilish release her first E.P. Don't Smile at Me?

A) 2015
B) 2016
C) 2017
D) 2018

21. Which track from *When We All Fall Asleep, Where Do We Go?* Became a fan favorite for its eerie sound?

A) Bad Guy
B) Bury a Friend
C) Xanny
D) I Love You

85: She Earned $53 Million in One Year

In 2020, Billie made Forbes' list of highest-paid celebrities, earning an eye-popping $53 million that year alone! From her massively successful world tour to her booming music sales and a huge deal with Apple, Billie's earnings skyrocketed. At such a young age, she became one of the top-earning musicians on the planet. What would you do with that kind of money? For Billie, it's not just about the cash—she's also been known to give back to causes she cares about, like environmental sustainability and animal rights. Talk about using success to make a difference!

86: Her Fans Helped Her Win the Guinness World Record for Most Simultaneous Charting Songs

Billie Eilish holds the Guinness World Record for the most simultaneous entries on the Billboard Hot 100 chart by a female artist. How did she do it? Thanks to her loyal and dedicated fans, her debut album When We All Fall Asleep, Where Do We Go? became an instant smash hit. An incredible 14 of her songs charted at the same time, proving just how much people loved her music. It's amazing to think about how much support she gets from her fans all over the world. How cool is it to have fans that help you break world records?

87: Billie Signed Her First Record Deal at 14 Years Old

At just 14, when most teenagers are busy with homework and hanging out with friends, Billie Eilish was signing her first record deal with Interscope Records! Her early song "Ocean Eyes" had already gone viral, grabbing the attention of major record labels. It wasn't long before she sealed the deal and started her rise to fame. Can you imagine being signed to a huge record label before even finishing high school? Talk about impressive! This was the start of what would become a career full of incredible accomplishments for Billie. Wouldn't it be wild to sign a record deal at such a young age?

88: Billie Loves Thrift Shopping

While Billie is known for wearing designer brands like Gucci, she's also a huge fan of thrift shopping! She has said in interviews that she loves finding unique and one-of-a-kind pieces in secondhand stores. It's a fun reminder that you don't have to wear all expensive clothes to create your own unique style. What's the coolest thing you've ever found while thrifting?

Did you know?

89: She Turned Down a Role in a Major Hollywood Film

Believe it or not, Billie Eilish was offered a role in a major Hollywood film early in her career. While she loves acting, she decided to turn it down to focus on her music. It's wild to think that she could have been on the big screen, but her dedication to her music paid off. Would you have taken the role or stuck with your passion like Billie?

90: Billie Eilish Has a Collection of 100+ Frog Jewelry Pieces

Did you know Billie Eilish has a fun and quirky obsession with frogs? It's true! Billie loves frogs so much that she's built an entire jewelry collection around them, with over 100 pieces of frog-themed jewelry. From cute rings to detailed necklaces, her collection is packed with these little amphibians. It's not just about the look—it's a playful way for Billie to express her unique style and personality. Frogs might not be your typical fashion statement, but that's what makes Billie so cool—she embraces the unexpected!

91: Billie Performed at the Global Citizen Festival

In 2021, Billie Eilish performed at the Global Citizen Festival, a global event raising awareness for climate change, poverty, and inequality. Billie joined other artists using their platforms to promote change. Her performance was part of a larger campaign to motivate leaders and governments to focus on solutions. Billie's passion for environmental causes is well-known, as she uses her influence to promote sustainability. Her appearance at Global Citizen further established her as a musician and a voice for social justice.

92: She Performed "No Time to Die" at the 2020 Brit Awards

Billie performed her James Bond theme song "No Time to Die" at the 2020 Brit Awards. Her brother Finneas accompanied this performance on piano and included an orchestra. The performance was widely praised and marked a significant moment in her career, reinforcing her status as one of the most versatile young artists in the industry.

93: Billie Eilish Has a Secret Talent for Acrobatics

Did you know that Billie Eilish has a hidden talent for acrobatics? Yep, as a kid, Billie was super into physical activities and could pull off flips, tricks, and moves that would make any gymnast proud. Although she doesn't showcase her acrobatic skills much anymore, it's fun to think about Billie doing cartwheels and handstands backstage before her shows. Can you picture her flipping through the air before hitting the stage? It's just another example of how Billie's talents go beyond music! What secret talent do you have that might surprise people?

94: She Released a Song in Collaboration with an Environmental Campaign

Billie Eilish doesn't just make waves in music—she's also passionate about saving the planet! In 2020, Billie collaborated with a campaign dedicated to raising awareness about Australia's Great Barrier Reef. Her hit song "Ocean Eyes" became the soundtrack to this cause, helping to educate people about the damage being done to this natural wonder. Using her music to inspire change shows how Billie combines her creativity with causes she truly cares about. Have you ever thought about using your own talents to make a difference in the world?

95: Billie Eilish Is an Avid Reader

Did you know Billie Eilish loves to read? While most people know her for her music, Billie has often mentioned how much she enjoys getting lost in a good book. She's particularly fond of novels that dive deep into complex characters and emotional stories. Reading gives her a way to unwind and get inspired creatively. Can you imagine Billie cozying up with a book just like any other bookworm? What's your favorite book—maybe you and Billie have similar tastes in reading!

96: Billie Eilish Keeps Her Love Life Private

While Billie Eilish is an open book about many things in her life, when it comes to her love life, she prefers to keep things private. Billie has mentioned in interviews that she values her personal space and doesn't feel the need to share every detail with the world. She wants to keep some parts of her life just for herself, away from the spotlight. It's a refreshing reminder that even superstars need privacy. How would you feel if you were in the public eye—would you keep some things just for yourself too?

22. Billie Eilish performed at which famous awards show's In Memoriam segment in 2020?

A) The Grammys
B) The Oscars
C) The Golden Globes
D) The MTV VMAs

23. What year did Billie win her first Grammy Award?

A) 2018
B) 2019
C) 2020
D) 2021

24. What was the theme of Billie's 2021 album Happier Than Ever?

A) Teenage love
B) Coping with fame
C) Personal growth and empowerment
D) Heartbreak

97: She Designed Eco-Friendly Merchandise for Her 2022 Tour

During her Happier Than Ever tour, Billie committed to environmental sustainability by offering eco-friendly merchandise. The products were made from recycled materials, and she partnered with eco-conscious brands to minimize the environmental impact of her tour. Billie has consistently used her platform to raise awareness for climate change and sustainable living.

98: Billie Eilish Is a Fan of "The Twilight Saga"

Though known for her edgy persona, Billie Eilish revealed she was a huge fan of The Twilight Saga. Growing up, Billie enjoyed books and movies, which was a big part of her teenage years. She's joked in interviews about being "Team Edward," showing her relatable side. Billie's admiration for the series connects her with fans who grew up obsessed with the same pop culture phenomenon. Even as a global superstar, Billie remains open about her childhood interests, showing that she, too, was once obsessed with fictional characters.

Did you know?

99: She Was a Big Believer in Aliens as a Kid

As a kid, Billie was fascinated by the idea of aliens and the unknown. She used to talk about what it would be like to encounter extraterrestrial life and spent time imagining the possibilities of otherworldly beings. It's fun to think about how Billie's creative imagination has always been a part of who she is. What do you think—are aliens out there?

100: Her Parents Helped Shape Her Career

Billie's parents, Maggie Baird and Patrick O'Connell, played a crucial role in shaping her career. Not only did they encourage Billie and Finneas to explore their creative talents, but they also contributed to their children's music careers by helping them with recording and production. Billie credits her close-knit family for keeping her grounded despite her massive success.

101: Billie Gave Away All of Her First Grammy Awards to Her Family

When Billie Eilish won her first Grammy Awards in 2020, she made a super sweet gesture—she gave them all away to her family! Billie said that her success was a family effort, so each family member got to keep a Grammy statue. How cool would it be to have a Grammy sitting on your family's mantel?

Billie Trivia!

25. Billie Eilish has cited which artist as a major influence on her music and style?

A) Lana Del Rey
B) Beyoncé
C) Adele
D) Lady Gaga

26. In which song does Billie Eilish explore the pressures of fame and self-image?

A) My Future
B) Bad Guy
C) Not My Responsibility
D) Ocean Eyes

27. Billie Eilish was the youngest artist to win which major Grammy category in 2020?

A) Record of the Year
B) Best New Artist
C) Album of the Year
D) Song of the Year

Billie Trivia!

28. Billie and her brother Finneas wrote a song for which animated film in 2022?

A) Turning Red
B) Encanto
C) Luca
D) Soul

29. Billie has been an advocate for which of these environmental causes?

A) Ocean Conservation
B) Veganism and animal rights
C) Renewable energy
D) Deforestation

30. Which Billie Eilish song has a music video featuring her covered in spiders?

A) Everything I Wanted
B) You Should See Me in a Crown
C) All the Good Girls Go to Hell
D) Bury a Friend

Billie Trivia!

31. What is the name of Billie Eilish's 2023 single featured in the Barbie movie soundtrack?

A) What Was I Made For?
B) Lost Cause
C) My Future
D) Your Power

32. Billie Eilish became the youngest headliner ever at which major UK festival?

A) Reading Festival
B) Glastonbury
C) Isle of Wight Festival
D) Leeds Festival

33. Which of Billie's albums was the first to top charts in multiple countries like U.S., U.K., and Australia?

A) Don't Smile at Me
B) When We All Fall Asleep, Where Do We Go?
C) Happier Than Ever
D) Hit Me Hard and Soft

Billie Trivia!

34. Billie's song "Everything I Wanted" is about which topic?

A) Overcoming nightmares
B) Personal struggles and insecurities
C) Dealing with fame
D) Losing loved ones

35. Billie Eilish grew up in which neighborhood of Los Angeles?

A) Hollywood
B) Silver Lake
C) Highland Park
D) Echo Park

36. Which artist did Billie collaborate with on the song "Lovely"?

A) Khalid
B) Charli XCX
C) Shawn Mendes
D) Halsey

Billie Trivia!

37. What was Billie's first collaboration with her brother Finneas?

A) Six Feet Under
B) Ocean Eyes
C) Bellyache
D) Watch

38. Which clothing style has Billie Eilish been known for throughout her career?

A) Formal and elegant
B) Bright neon colors
C) Oversized and baggy
D) Minimalist and plain

39. Billie's famous cover of which song by The Beatles gained widespread recognition?

A) Yesterday
B) Let It Be
C) Blackbird
D) Here Comes the Sun

Billie Trivia!

40. Which female artist did Billie praise during her 2020 Grammys speech?

A) Taylor Swift
B) Beyoncé
C) Ariana Grande
D) Adele

41. What is the title of Billie Eilish's debut E.P.?

A) When We All Fall Asleep, Where Do We Go?
B) Don't Smile at Me
C) Happier Than Ever
D) Six Feet Under

42. Billie Eilish recorded her debut single, "Ocean Eyes," for what purpose before it went viral?

A) As a gift for her mom
B) For her dance instructor's choreography
C) For a school project
D) For her acting audition

Billie Trivia!

43. What was the main theme of Billie's Happier Than Ever album?

A) Growing up in the spotlight
B) Navigating relationships and personal growth
C) Breaking away from societal expectations
D) Environmental activism

44. Billie performed at the 2020 Democratic National Convention to support which presidential candidate?

A) Bernie Sanders
B) Joe Biden
C) Elizabeth Warren
D) Kamala Harris

45. Billie Eilish worked with her brother Finneas to write three original songs for which animated film?

A) Moana
B) Turning Red
C) Frozen II
D) Soul

Billie Trivia!

46. In 2021, Billie Eilish was honored with a special vinyl album edition created using what material?

A) Gold-plated vinyl
B) Recycled vinyl scraps
C) Clear acrylic
D) Neon-colored vinyl

47. Billie Eilish made her acting debut in which satirical thriller series in 2023?

A) Swarm
B) Euphoria
C) The Idol
D) Stranger Things

48. What hair color is Billie Eilish most famously known for in her early career?

A) Blue
B) Black and green
C) Blonde
D) Red

Billie Trivia!

49. Which artist collaborated with Billie Eilish for her remix of the song "Bad Guy"?

A) Shawn Mendes
B) Justin Bieber
C) Drake
D) Post Malone

50. What is the name of Billie Eilish's fragrance brand launched in 2021?

A) Ocean Breeze
B) Sweet Dreams
C) Eilish
D) Glow

51. Billie and her brother Finneas wrote the song "No Time to Die." Which film series did they write for?

A) The Avengers
B) Star Wars
C) James Bond
D) The Hunger Games

Billie Trivia!

52. In what year did Billie Eilish first headline at the Coachella music festival?

A) 2019
B) 2020
C) 2022
D) 2021

53. Which Billie Eilish song discusses body image and society's expectations of women?

A) Bad Guy
B) All the Good Girls Go to Hell
C) Not My Responsibility
D) Everything I Wanted

54. Billie Eilish is known for advocating which cause is related to animals?

A) Protecting endangered species
B) Promoting veganism
C) Protesting animal testing in cosmetics
D) Saving marine life

Billie
Trivia!

55. Billie's album *Happier Than Ever* broke her record for the most pre-saved album on which platform?

A) Spotify
B) YouTube
C) Apple Music
D) Tidal

56. Billie released ___ in response to the 2022 Supreme Court decision overturning Roe v. Wade.

A) T.V.
B) Your Power
C) Happier Than Ever
D) My Future

57. What title did Billie earn in 2020 by Forbes due to her significant earnings?

A) Youngest Person of the Year
B) Highest-Earning Female Artist Under 30
C) Youngest Person on the Celebrity 100
D) Top-Earning Musician of the Year

Billie Trivia!

58. "No Time to Die" won an Academy Award in which year?

A) 2020
B) 2021
C) 2022
D) 2023

59. Billie Eilish released an eco-friendly limited-edition vinyl version of which album?

A) Don't Smile at Me
B) When We All Fall Asleep, Where Do We Go?
C) Happier Than Ever
D) Hit Me Hard and Soft

60. In which year did Billie Eilish become a brand ambassador for Gucci?

A) 2020
B) 2021
C) 2022
D) 2023

Billie Trivia!

61. What was the name of Billie Eilish's first music video she directed herself?

A) Xanny
B) Bad Guy
C) When the Party's Over
D) You Should See Me in a Crown

62. Billie Eilish shared that she has a condition that causes involuntary movements or sounds. What is it?

A) Epilepsy
B) Tourette syndrome
C) OCD
D) ADHD

63. What inspired Billie's viral song "Ocean Eyes"?

A) A movie she loved
B) Her dance instructor's choreography
C) A dream she had
D) A poem she wrote

Billie Trivia!

64. Which app played a significant role in Billie Eilish's rise to fame with "Ocean Eyes"?

A) Instagram
B) SoundCloud
C) TikTok
D) YouTube

65. Billie Eilish has won multiple Grammy Awards. What was the first year she won Record of the Year?

A) 2019
B) 2020
C) 2021
D) 2022

66. Besides her music career, Billie Eilish is known for promoting which type of lifestyle?

A) Veganism
B) Minimalism
C) Yoga
D) Meditation

Billie Trivia!

67. Billie Eilish performed the theme song for which James Bond movie?

A) Skyfall
B) Spectre
C) No Time to Die
D) Quantum of Solace

68. What is the name of Billie Eilish's live concert film released in 2023?

A) Happier Than Ever: A Love Letter to Los Angeles
B) Billie Eilish: The Live Experience
C) Where Do We Go? The Livestream
D) Happier Than Ever: The World Tour

69. Billie Eilish often uses her platform to raise awareness for which environmental cause?

A) Global warming
B) Coral reef protection
C) Deforestation
D) Ocean pollution

Billie Trivia!

70. Which famous pop star was one of Billie's early musical inspirations and later became a friend?

A) Katy Perry
B) Justin Bieber
C) Britney Spears
D) Selena Gomez

71. Billie Eilish made headlines at the Met Gala in 2021 by wearing a dress inspired by which iconic figure?

A) Marilyn Monroe
B) Audrey Hepburn
C) Grace Kelly
D) Elizabeth Taylor

72. What does Billie Eilish say inspired her "Everything I Wanted" song?

A) A nightmare
B) A personal relationship
C) Fan expectations
D) Her struggle with fame

Billie Trivia!

73. In 2022, Billie Eilish became the youngest-ever headliner of which iconic music festival?

A) Glastonbury
B) Coachella
C) Bonnaroo
D) Lollapalooza

74. Which fashion brand did Billie collaborate with to release a signature fragrance?

A) Gucci
B) Louis Vuitton
C) Chanel
D) None (She launched her own fragrance)

75. Billie Eilish voiced a character in a short film from which popular animated series?

A) The Simpsons
B) Family Guy
C) Lisa Simpson
D) South Park

Billie Trivia!

76. What is Billie's relationship with her older brother Finneas?

A) He is her manager
B) He is her producer and collaborator
C) He is her stylist
D) He is her social media manager

77. What inspired Billie's 2023 song "What Was I Made For?"?

A) A Barbie movie
B) Her personal experiences
C) A fan letter
D) A dream she had

78. Billie Eilish has a lifelong love for which outdoor activity?

A) Hiking
B) Skateboarding
C) Horseback riding
D) Surfing

Billie Trivia!

79. Which iconic pop star did Billie cover in a viral TikTok performance?

A) Britney Spears
B) Madonna
C) Harry Styles
D) Avril Lavigne

80. Who did Billie collaborate with on the remix of "Bad Guy"?

A) Justin Bieber
B) Khalid
C) Doja Cat
D) The Weeknd

81. What was the first song Billie Eilish performed live on tour?

A) Bad Guy
B) Ocean Eyes
C) Bellyache
D) Copycat

Billie Trivia!

82. Billie's song "My Future" was written during which significant world event?

A) The 2020 U.S. Election
B) The COVID-19 Pandemic
C) The 2021 Met Gala
D) Her 18th birthday

83. Billie Eilish collaborated with which film composer to create her James Bond theme song?

A) Hans Zimmer
B) Thomas Newman
C) John Williams
D) Ludwig Göransson

84. What role did Billie's mother play in her musical career?

A) Co-writer of her lyrics
B) Her vocal coach
C) Director of her music videos
D) Taught her and Finneas how to write songs

Billie
Trivia!

85. Which of Billie's songs includes a line referencing the pressures of fame?

A) Bad Guy
B) Everything I Wanted
C) Your Power
D) My Future

86. Billie Eilish became the first artist born in the 21st century to do what?

A) Release a diamond-certified single
B) Top the Billboard 200
C) Perform at the Super Bowl
D) Win an Academy Award

87. What was the unique feature of Billie's Happier Than Ever album release in 2021?

A) It was released with a documentary
B) It had an eco-friendly vinyl edition
C) It included fan collaborations
D) It was performed live on launch day

Billie Trivia!

88. Billie's older brother Finneas received Grammy recognition for what role in her career?

A) Songwriting
B) Vocal producing
C) Mixing and mastering
D) Playing guitar on tour

89. Which environmental cause did Billie Eilish advocate for during her Happier Than Ever tour?

A) Protecting the rainforest
B) Reducing plastic waste
C) Ocean Conservation
D) Reforestation efforts

90. In 2024, Billie Eilish appeared as a guest star in which popular T.V. series?

A) Stranger Things
B) Swarm
C) Euphoria
D) The Mandalorian

Billie Trivia!

91. Billie Eilish made her debut performance at which music award show?

A) The Grammys
B) The American Music Awards
C) The MTV Video Music Awards
D) The Billboard Music Awards

92. What iconic late-night show did Billie Eilish first perform on?

A) The Tonight Show with Jimmy Fallon
B) Saturday Night Live
C) The Late Late Show with James Corden
D) Jimmy Kimmel Live!

93. What is the title of Billie Eilish's 2022 world tour?

A) When We All Fall Asleep Tour
B) Where Do We Go? World Tour
C) Happier Than Ever World Tour
D) Don't Smile at Me Tour

Billie Trivia!

94. Billie collaborated with Pixar to write songs for which animated film?

A) Inside Out
B) Turning Red
C) Soul
D) Onward

95. Billie's first viral hit, "Ocean Eyes," was originally written for what purpose?

A) Her debut album
B) A school project
C) A dance performance
D) A soundtrack

96. Billie Eilish's middle name, Pirate, was chosen by who?

A) Her mother
B) Her brother
C) Her father
D) Her aunt

Billie Trivia!

97. Which of these artists did Billie cite as one of her biggest style influences?

A) Madonna
B) Avril Lavigne
C) Beyonce
D) Rihanna

98. Billie Eilish performed a tribute song for which late music legend at the 2020 Oscars?

A) David Bowie
B) Prince
C) Kobe Bryant
D) Whitney Houston

99. Billie Eilish directed which of her own music videos for the first time?

A) Xanny
B) Everything I Wanted
C) Bad Guy
D) Happier Than Ever

Billie Trivia!

100. Billie Eilish was the youngest-ever headliner for which music festival?

A) Lollapalooza
B) Coachella
C) Glastonbury
D) Bonnaroo

101. What notable trait does Billie Eilish's dog, Shark, have?

A) He is a pit bull
B) He was adopted from a shelter
C) He stars in her music videos
D) Both A and B

Answers!

1. A) Ocean Eyes
2. D) Her brother Finneas
3. C) 2019
4. B) No Time to Die
5. B) Academy Award
6. A) Pirate
7. C) Justin Bieber
8. C) Coachella
9. B) Happier Than Ever
10. D) Los Angeles
11. B) Tourette syndrome
12. B) Finneas
13. A) Bad Guy
14. B) By - Billie Eilish
15. A) 14
16. C) Four
17. B) Classic Rock
18. A) Shark
19. C) Billie Eilish: The World's a Little Blurry
20. B) 2016
21. B) Bury a Friend
22. B) The Oscars
23. C) 2020
24. C) Personal growth and empowerment
25. A) Lana Del Rey
26. C) Not My Responsibility
27. A) Record of the Year
28. A) Turning Red
29. B) Veganism and animal rights
30. B) You Should See Me in a Crown
31. A) What Was I Made For?
32. B) Glastonbury
33. B) When We All Fall Asleep, Where Do We Go?
34. C) Dealing with fame
35. C) Highland Park

Answers!

36. A) Khalid
37. B) Ocean Eyes
38. C) Oversized and baggy
39. C) Blackbird
40. C) Ariana Grande
41. B) Don't Smile at Me
42. B) For her dance instructor's choreography
43. B) Navigating relationships and personal growth
44. B) Joe Biden
45. B) Turning Red
46. B) Recycled vinyl scraps
47. A) Swarm
48. B) Black and green
49. B) Justin Bieber
50. C) Eilish
51. C) James Bond
52. C) 2022
53. C) Not My Responsibility
54. B) Promoting veganism
55. A) Spotify
56. A) T.V.
57. C) Youngest Person on the Celebrity 100
58. C) 2022
59. C) Happier Than Ever
60. A) 2020
61. A) Xanny
62. B) Tourette syndrome
63. B) Her dance instructor's choreography
64. B) SoundCloud
65. B) 2020
66. A) Veganism
67. C) No Time to Die
68. A) Happier Than Ever: A Love Letter to Los Angeles

Answers!

69. D) Ocean pollution
70. B) Justin Bieber
71. A) Marilyn Monroe
72. A) A nightmare
73. A) Glastonbury
74. D) None (She launched her own fragrance, Eilish)
75. A) The Simpsons
76. B) He is her producer and collaborator
77. A) A Barbie movie
78. B) Skateboarding
79. D) Avril Lavigne
80. A) Justin Bieber
81. B) Ocean Eyes
82. B) The COVID-19 Pandemic
83. A) Hans Zimmer
84. D) Taught her and Finneas how to write songs
85. B) Everything I Wanted
86. D) Win an Academy Award
87. B) It had an eco-friendly vinyl edition
88. A) Songwriting
89. B) Reducing plastic waste
90. B) Swarm
91. C) The MTV Video Music Awards
92. B) Saturday Night Live
93. C) Happier Than Ever World Tour
94. B) Turning Red
95. C) A dance performance
96. B) Her brother
97. B) Avril Lavigne
98. C) Kobe Bryant
99. A) Xanny
100. B) Coachella
101. D) Both A and B

20-39: Billie Beginner-in-the-Making

You're just getting started in the world of Billie Eilish! You've picked up some cool facts, and you're beginning to understand what makes her so special. Keep listening to her music and learning about her journey —there's so much more to discover! With a little more digging, you'll be well on your way to becoming a Billie expert!

40-59: Billie Rising Star

You're doing great! You've got a solid grip on Billie's music and story, and your passion for her work is really shining through. You know some key details, and it's clear you're almost at the next level. Keep it up— you're so close to joining the ranks of the true Billie superfans!

60-79: Billie Enthusiast Extraordinaire

Wow, you've really immersed yourself in Billie's world! You know way more than just the basics—you've explored her life, her music, and even some hidden facts. You're just a step away from becoming a true expert. Keep going, you're super close to mastering all things Billie!

80-100: Billie Eilish Legend

Congrats! You're officially a Billie Eilish Legend! You know her career, life, and music inside out. Your knowledge is unmatched, and you've truly reached the highest level of Billie fandom. You've not just learned the facts—you've become part of her story. Keep being amazing, because you're a legend, just like Billie!

Dear Billie know it all 😉,

Thank you so much for joining me on this fun ride through "101 Facts About Billie Eilish: The Unofficial Kid and Teen Quiz & Trivia Guide to the Pop Music Sensation."

Having you read along has made this project even more special!

Putting this book together was such a blast. Learning all these cool facts about Billie and seeing how much she inspires others was awesome. Every fact in here is a little piece of what makes her journey so amazing.

This book was created with love, and it's meant to bring fans who admire Billie's talent and story together! Let us and others know what this book meant for you by scanning this QR code and writing a review!

Enjoy the coloring section :)

P.S this is me up the top left, until next time,

Tessa Temecula

I have added a QR code with the coloring pages that come along with the paperback.

I have also added a downloadable PDF if you would like to print out the book for you and your friends :)

If you are also Interested in Taylor Swift, Dolly Parton, Beyonce or Olivia Rodrigo and want a digital copy of the book, email us at 101factsaboutstars@gmail.com for more details!

Thank you,

Tessa Temecula

What Fear Will You Face?

Billie has always talked about facing her fears, like in her spooky "Bury a Friend" music video. What's something you've been afraid to do but want to face head-on? Write about a fear you have and how you think you can overcome it. What's your first step? You've got this—Billie would totally cheer you on!

Your "Ocean Eyes" Moment

Billie's song "Ocean Eyes" was her big break, and it all started when she shared it with the world. Have you ever had a moment where you felt like you did something amazing or brave? Write about a time you felt proud of yourself, just like Billie did with her music. How did it make you feel? What's your "Ocean Eyes" moment?

What's Your Power Song?

Billie's song "Happier Than Ever" is all about feeling strong and standing up for yourself. Write about a time when you felt powerful, like nothing could stop you. What helped you feel that way? If you had a power song, what would it be called?

Your "Everything I Wanted" Dream

In "Everything I Wanted," Billie sings about getting everything she ever dreamed of but feeling overwhelmed by it. What's something you've always wanted, and how would you feel if you got it? Write about your biggest dream and how you imagine your life would change if it came true.

Your Dream Collaboration

Billie has worked with so many amazing artists—like her brother Finneas! If you could work with anyone, who would it be? Whether it's a musician, a writer, or even your best friend, write about your dream collaboration. What would you create together? How fun would that be?

What's in Your Future?

In "My Future," Billie talks about being hopeful and excited for what's next. What are YOU looking forward to in your future? Write about your biggest dreams and the goals you have. What steps can you take today to start making those dreams come true?

Your Go-To Billie Song

What's your favorite Billie Eilish song, and why does it speak to you? Maybe it helped you through a tough time or just makes you feel happy. Write about the song that means the most to you and how it makes you feel every time you hear it. What's your Billie anthem?

Create Your Big Dream

Billie and her brother wrote their first hit song when they were teens. If you could create something amazing—like a song, story, or art—what would it be? Write about your big idea and how you would make it happen. What would you need? Who would help you?

How Will You Speak Up?

Billie always uses her platform to speak out about important issues like mental health, body positivity, and the environment. If you could use your voice for something important, what would it be? Write about what matters most to you and how you can speak up about it.

Create Your Feel-Good Playlist

Billie's music can match any mood—whether you're feeling sad, happy, or anything in between. If you could create a playlist for your feelings right now, what songs would be on it? Include some Billie tracks, of course! Write out your playlist and explain why each song made the cut.

Why Being Honest is Your Strength

Billie isn't afraid to be real and vulnerable in her music. Think about a time when being open and honest helped you or someone else. Write about why showing your true self makes you stronger. How can you be more real in your everyday life?

Celebrate What Makes You Different

Billie embraces her unique style and creativity—she's all about being herself. What makes YOU unique? Write about the things that make you different, whether it's your style, hobbies, or personality. How can you celebrate those differences every day?

Boost Your Confidence

Billie wears clothes that make her feel comfortable and in control—how awesome is that? What makes YOU feel confident? Write about a time when you felt proud and powerful. What gave you that confidence? How can you hold onto that feeling more often?

Made in the USA
Middletown, DE
22 December 2024

68081263R00066